The GameChanger Perspective

by Mr. Oscar J. Starr III

DORRANCE
PUBLISHING CO
EST. 1920
PITTSBURGH, PENNSYLVANIA 15238

Dorrance Publishing Co
585 Alpha Drive
Pittsburgh, PA 15238
Visit our website at *www.dorrancebookstore.com*

ISBN: 979-8-89341-811-8
eISBN: 979-8-8881-2524-3

The GameChanger Perspective
Table of contents

Chapter One: What Is a Game-Changer?

We are going to take a look in what it takes to be a real game-changer, the definition as well as the perspective viewpoint. Bringing an understanding it's interpretation and the evidence that's proven itself.

What is a Game-Changer?

The term game-changer refers to an individual or company, that significantly alters the way things are done as a whole. Individual game-changers find a way to stand out by way of their personality.

Game-changing companies are able to switch things up and form new business plans and strategies that place them above their competitors. By mere virtue of their actions, game-changers can make changes that transform the landscape as a whole.

A game-changer is an individual or company that significantly alters the way things are done as a whole.

Game-changing individuals often use their personality traits and attitude to spark change.

Companies that are game-changers look for new and innovative business plans, efficiencies, production methods, and marketing strategies.

Becoming a game-changer requires time, determination, and the ability to ride out any uncertainties.

Understanding Game-Changers

Game-changing is the ability to make significant changes. These changes may often be radical, but almost always lead to a shift in the way others think and do things. A game-changer, therefore, is someone or something that can spark a great deal of change.

Chapter Two: Distinctive Traits of a Game-Changer

A game-changing individual often uses their personality traits and attitude to change the way people think and how others do things. These people are often called *influencers*, because they can shift the dynamic and change the way people think and act.

For instance, a *social media* influencer with one million followers may be considered a game-changer because of their fashion sense. As such, they are able to revolutionize how others dress.

Game-changing companies are those that look for new business plans, efficiencies, production methods, and marketing strategies. These innovations open up new avenues of economic and financial growth, often transforming the entire image of an industry.

Companies are often headed up by game-changing individuals—visionary leaders with game-changing ideas continue to create innovative new paths to change the status quo. Becoming a game-changer requires long-term commitment as well as innovative thinking.

Reaching game-changing levels requires long-term commitment—one that takes time, determination, and the ability to ride out uncertainties that may arise. But entrepreneurs can find new tactics, ways of thinking, or other characteristics that make up a game-changer or industry disruptor, by learning from other leadership and understanding the anatomy of game-changing companies.

Examples of Game-Changers

Jeff Bezos

Billionaire and Amazon founder Jeff Bezos is widely recognized as a game-changer. It's not surprising when you consider what he's done since he founded the company in 1994. Amazon started as a little book e-commerce website during the internet boom of the late 1990s, quickly disrupting the retail industry as a whole.

Bezos stepped down from the role of CEO on July 5, 2021, but remains executive chair of the company. Bezos continues to invest in new game-changing technologies, such as spaceflight.

Elon Musk

Elon Musk is another entrepreneurial individual who is considered to be a game-changer. Musk, who became Tesla's CEO in 2008, had high ambitions of being a game-changer in the auto industry.

Tesla is now the leading name in electric cars, bringing them into the modern world by using high-powered lithium-ion batteries to power vehicles rather than gasoline. While Musk's vision for Tesla production is often criticized, the company's emergence in the electric car market is causing others to scramble and try to catch up to its impressive lead.

Chapter Three: Becoming A Game-Changer in Business

What is a game-changer in business? Let us take a look in what it defines especially in the business industry.

Here's my definition: A game-changer is someone who introduces something with so much added value that their competitors want to become customers.

The game-changers are the one who break beyond the traditional confines of business and become immensely successful at whatever they do. They not only dominate their niche, they define it by becoming the go-to company, service, expert, or influencer.

And if you're wondering why I'm qualified to be talking about the idea of a game changer, it's because I spent years learning how to change my own game.

This not something that happens overnight, but it is something you can consciously work toward if you understand how game changers are made. So, let's take a look at what it means to be a game-changer in business and what it takes to be one.

Game-changers are comfortable with breaking norms.

If you want to introduce something so revolutionary that you're able to turn your competitors into customers, you're going to need to break some norms and think outside the box. Game-changers come up with outlandish ideas and pursue them even when everyone else thinks they're crazy.

Game-changers don't fight back.

When game-changers come up with these outlandish ideas, they're usually met with the devil's advocate. Everyone tells them they're crazy, their idea won't work, and their business is going to fail.

As human beings, our natural instinct is to fight back in these situations. We argue and try to prove our point. But the real game-changers understand that fighting isn't worth their time. You don't get very far by doing that, and nothing of value comes out of it.

Game-changers aren't concerned whether people think their ideas are outlandish or crazy. It doesn't change their thinking, and it doesn't change the fact that they will relentlessly pursue their goals and ideas to get where they want to go. If anything, it fuels them!

Game-changers welcome obstacles.

When most people hit obstacles, they get discouraged or give up entirely.

Game-changers understand that obstacles are the raw material that creates the road map to success. They welcome obstacles because that means they're on the right path. After all, if there were no obstacles, then everyone would be a game changer.

Overcoming obstacles is just the natural progression for game changers. They face obstacles throughout their lives, but they understand the value of them. Overcoming obstacles makes you and your business stronger; it makes the end result that much more valuable.

Question: What is a business without obstacles, after all? The reality is that businesses that don't encounter any obstacles are ordinary, mediocre, and only mildly successful. Businesses that encounter many obstacles (and overcome them) are the true game-changers. Those are the ones that become **wildly successful** and ubiquitous, and dominate their niche.

When game-changers have no obstacles in their path, they see a problem. And when there are obstacles, they welcome them-because obstacles energize them, encourage them, and guide them.

So when we ask ourselves, "What is a game changer in business?" most of us already know the answer....

The game-changers are the ones who do what everyone is **unwilling** to do. They break norms, they welcome adversity, and they see obstacles for what they really are: fuel to get where they want to go.

Chapter Four: The Game-Changer Entrepreneur

I've been working with entrepreneurs for more than two years, and my favorite type of entrepreneur to work with is a **Game-Changer.** These are entrepreneurs who are so freed up with the pressures of time and money that they can see and continually set up their entrepreneurial life as a game—one they can win and enjoy.

Cash Versus Creativity

I've come across two very different types of entrepreneurs over the course of my coaching career. The first what I call a "cash player." Cash players are interested in money—and not much else. If presented with an idea to create or be a part of something new, they write it off if they can't see how money is going to come in right away. This is fine, and cash players are necessary in the marketplace, but they're not the type of entrepreneur I'm interested in working with.

The other type of entrepreneur, and the type I much prefer to work with, is what I identify as a "creativity player." These entrepreneurs are fascinated by the process of putting things together to create something new. They're confident in their money-making abilities, so they trust that they'll make money on their new ideas somewhere down the road, but that's not their first consideration.

They're interested in creative partnerships, creative teamwork, and creative breakthroughs. Creativity players may still use money to keep score, but the game is about something much bigger for them. It's about growth.

What I've discovered is that all the Game-Changer entrepreneurs I've encountered creativity players not cash players.

Passion

The work Game-Changers do is a real expression of who they are. It comes from the inside. They get enormous amounts of meaning and purpose from their work and feel very strongly that they're creating something of great value.

They make money in a way that stimulates and motivates them, and they recognize that they can continually increase the energizing aspect of their careers, making it so that they never want to retire.

Game-Changers don't see other entrepreneurs as competition but instead jump at opportunities to combine their unique skills with somebody else's unique skills to create something new and unique in the marketplace.

People

For Game-Changers, their work is all people-based, and we're not talking about millions of people liking what they do. Game-Changers think in terms of specific individuals. They've became so good at getting inside the heads of their favorite customers or clients, that they can see the world through the eyes of the people who will benefit from their game-changing idea.

Their first instinct is to consider, "Is this really helping this person? Is it transforming the game that my customer or client is able to play?"

Permission

Entrepreneurism can be a lonely business. At the start, it requires you to depart from how the general population does things, and that's something you need to give yourself permission to do if it's the road you desire to take.

For an entrepreneur to jump into the Game-Changer game, it requires another level of permission, and that's for them to use their passion to transform the lives of particular people in the marketplace in a new way.

Entrepreneurs are unique in their ability to create their own game, yet even some very successful entrepreneurs don't realize that they have the freedom and ability to do this. Game-Changers have realized it, and they've learned to continually design a game that keeps them fascinated and motivated, and becomes the foundation for achieving all of their evolving life goals.

If you're wondering how you measure up, start by asking yourself these questions:

Are you passionate about something you've created?

Do you have a clear idea of the people who are going to be transformed by your new idea, and does the idea of being a hero to them excite you?

Do you give yourself permission to play this game for the rest of your life?

If you can confidently answer yes to all three, then you're a part of an elite group of Game-Changer entrepreneurs who are making a continued contribution, altering the marketplace, and transforming their industries.

Chapter Five: The Entrepreneurial Characteristics

Think you have the entrepreneurial characteristics? Some are natural, some are learned, but all of these traits are important for success.

They're passionate.

Successful entrepreneurs have a passion for what they do. Whether it is a brand-new invention, an improvement on an existing product, or a revolutionary service, successful entrepreneurs believe that their offering is game-changing, and they know why. They also know how to convey this passion to others.

They're business savvy.

As an entrepreneur, you will need to do everything in your business, at least at the beginning. Even as you grow and hire staff, you'll still want to know what's going on in accounting, marketing, purchasing, and everywhere else.

If you don't already have this knowledge, a business degree can be immensely helpful. A specialized degree program can teach you about all aspects of business, giving you a broad foundation to build on. At some schools, you can even specialize in entrepreneurship to help you get your dreams off the ground. Having all the knowledge that a business degree provides can help you make sure your new venture goals get off to the best possible start.

They're confident.

Confidence is one of the key characteristics of an entrepreneur. This one goes hand in hand with passion. True entrepreneurs believe that they have the ability to bring their product to market.

Sometimes this means trying a new approach if the first one doesn't work, as well as having the ability to overcome the obstacles that will inevitably come your way.

They're planners.

We've all heard the expression, "Nobody plans to fail, they just fail to plan." Nowhere is this more true than when starting a business. It's nearly impossible to over-plan. That said, be prepared for your plans to change. Entrepreneurs need to be flexible enough to discard a plan that proves unworkable and exchange it for another one.

They're money managers.

Being able to manage money is an important characteristic of an entrepreneur. Having a business degree can give you enough of a foundation in accounting and finance to manage the money yourself at the beginning. But if this isn't on your list of strong suits, make it the first thing that you outsource. It's way too important to be ignored while you focus on other priorities.

They never give up.

Bringing a product or service to the marketplace is a lot of hard work. Since you have passion and confidence already, it may not seem like you do, but there will come times when you think you've done all you can.

That's when you have to pull yourself back up, call on the knowledge, expertise, passion, and commitment you have, and give it one more shot.

Chapter Six: Evidence of A Game-Changer

How can you recognize a game-changer in your company? Even better, how can you honestly evaluate yourself to determine if you are a game changer?

Examples of evidence to evaluate yourself as a game-changer. Evidence #1: You are an expert in your field.

The second king of Israel wrote in the tenth century BC: "Do you see a man skilled in his work? He will stand before kings; He will not stand before obscure men." Game-changers have tendencies to be highly immersed in the area of their expertise. They are not only continuous students of their occupation field but also teachers (sharers of information) and great partners to their peer group.

Challenge yourself

When was the last time someone asked for your expert advice or asked to create something that was viewed important and critical? Do leaders in your organization share information with you and ask for your opinion? Are you a "wanted person" in your community? Or is what you know easily learned by searching Google?

Game-changers believe that some things are absolutely right, and some very wrong. They know the difference when someone misspeaks as opposed to lies. They observe and seek those who plan for greater good versus those who scheme for selfish reasons. Because of that, they firmly seek strategic views and hold firm beliefs of what needs to be accomplished.

They are seekers of truth, and they cling to it even at a high cost. As Martin Luther King once said: "I believe that unarmed truth and unconditional love will have the final word in reality. This is why right, temporarily defeated, is stronger than evil triumphant." Game-changers believe in absolute good, and they are willing to endure injustice for it.

Evidence #2: You are not afraid to lose what you have.

I remember listening to the story, I believe written by Brazilian author Paulo Coelho, who describes a ship caught in such a fierce storm that sailors couldn't do anything but hold on to save their lives. It was one of those seventeenth-century ship armed with cannons.

At one point, one of the cannons got loose and was hitting both sides of the ship as the ship swung from one side to another. Sailors were holding on for their lives but realized that soon, the loose cannon would create a hole in the ship, and they would die.

The question was obvious: "Who is going to let go, risk their life, and secure the cannon in this storm." The brave man who let go to save the ship was a **game-changer.**

We see it all the time in corporate America. Folks that manage to stay out of conflict, just enough to convince people that they are easy to work with. They do just what they the public square that nothing to say and "even a fool is considered wise as long as he keeps his mouth shut." They are afraid they will lose the position they waited for so long to obtain. So they don't lead, and they don't take risks or innovate. Eventually, they will arrive at the point in their career that they feared the most-becoming irrelevant.

Challenge yourself

Next time you see injustice done at work, or people spreading lies, will you stand for those unfairly affected?

Evidence #3: You are not liked by everyone.

Funny, as I was writing this book, my children were listening to the radio, and a song came on the radio with the lyrics that started like this: "Isn't it amazing how a man can find himself alone...He climbs on up the hill...He looks back at the crowd and says 'I am difference maker.'"

Apostle Paul wrote over two thousand years ago to make every effort to live in peace with all, but he never assumed he would be liked along the way. He knew better. Difference-makers make change. The majority of people don't like change. Herein lies the conflict, especially to those who will lose financial, social, or any other influence for change. Game-changers often find themselves alone, abandoned by others, yet it is their lives we celebrate throughout history.

Challenge yourself

Do you claim to be a balanced person who can work with anyone?

Admiral Grace Hopper once said: *"The most important thing I've accomplished is training young people. They come to me, you know, and say, 'Do you think we can do this?' I say, 'Try it.' And I back 'em up They need that. I keep track of them as they get older and I stir 'em up at intervals so they don't forget to take chances."*

Game-changers care about people and their progress. They teach, support, and build into others. They don't do it for the money, or recognition, but simply because they love people. After all, true game-changers know that everything they have, they received; so they simply pay forward. Down deep inside, game know they were meant to serve people.

Challenge yourself

Is there anyone in your life that could use your help today? Do you believe that people need help regardless of their circumstances?

Conclusion

Some of the questions that are not easy to honestly answer. But remember, nobody takes medicine unless they don't think something is wrong with them; and no game-changer fights for change if they everything is right in the world. The first step in being a game changer is to honestly evaluate yourself and others.

There are game-changers out there that are shaping our lives. ***Are you one of them?***

Chapter Seven: Game-Changers That Make a Positive Impact

In our work, we've come across a few Game-Changers, as we like to call them, are people who will not accept a mediocre way of doing business. They don't fear change; rather, they see it as a necessity for growth.

Game-Changers are aware of their impact on their people and leverage this to implement new, sometimes subtle ways of doing things. They lead through example and their desire for more outweighs their fear of failure.

Game-Changers are bold enough to shake things up and play differently, to win. They also recognize that to win, you need people on your side.

Resistance to change is prevalent in all organizations and inherently within people. We are creatures of habit. When sometimes threatens our safety and stability, we feel vulnerable. Our minds and bodies tell us something in the environment is jeopardizing our safety, so we freeze and ward off any attack. We resist change!

Only when we begin to understand and rationalize change and to recognize that it is for us—along with our teams and organizations—do we buy into it and commit to what needs to be done to change. As leaders, it is our job to be effective Change-Makers by being successful ***Game-Changers.***

How to be a successful Game-Changer

Know your impact. To change the rules of the game, Game-Changers are clear about the reason for and impact that of the change and communicate this with their people. They are clear about how the benefits outweigh the effort; and that there is a ***real***

need for change. Without this, resistance persists, and buy-in commitment is less likely. Game-Changers are clear about what footprints they will leave behind.

Address your Capability Gap. The truth is that we are not superheroes. We don't know it all, nor we are highly skilled at everything. In the same way that authentic leaders show vulnerability while still saving face, Game-Changers address any capability gaps related to the change to be successful. When we are clear about our shortcomings, we are better able to predict and foresee future outcomes, and fear the unknown tends to diminish.

Resistance is less likely to occur when employees feel that their leaders can competently and confidently manage the change—ironically, competence and confidence breeds when we have a keen awareness of our capability gaps.

Don't be a Hoarder. Out with the old, in with the new. If the old isn't working for you anymore, why are you still holding on to it? Game-Changers recognize when it's time to let go of a system or procedure and do so without regret. If it's the wrong fit for who you are and what you do now, cut the strings and innovate. Game-Changers challenge people out of their comfort zones and are brave enough to disrupt those hardwired connections to the old ways.

Abide by the Golden Rule. Game-Changers do not lead exclusively—they lead amongst the *pack.* For this reason, Game-Changers treat others in the way they wish to be treated. In dealing with change, Game-Changers communicate clearly and continuously. They make efforts to inform employees and to keep them in the know, in order to have them both body and heart through the transition.

What is it that you want to do differently this year? What will you keep, change, or throw out the window? What do you need to accept in order to let go of? While change doesn't happen overnight, or need to be revolutionary, change comes about by making small steps on new pathways that lead to a new or existing goal. Are you courageous enough to be a ***Game-Changer?***

Chapter Eight: Creating A Game-Changer

A game-changer is that ah-ha moment where you see something others don't. It's the transformational magic that takes organizations from ordinary to exceptional.

Relentless Pursuit

Ever wonder how people come up with the proverbial big idea? They work at it. Put simply, the best leaders proactively focus on pursuing game-changers. They're never satisfied with the ordinary or mundane. Richard Branson, Jeff Bezos, and other CEOs recognized for their big ideas didn't just get lucky—they were and are committed to the constant pursuit of game changers. They aren't just dreamers—they are doers. Successful leaders are nothing if not persistent, committed individuals who understand potential is of little value if said potential fails to be realized.

Be Original

One of the things that's wrong with today's marketplace is there's too much rehashing of old ideas spun as new. Great leaders aren't copycats; they abhor *me too* business methodologies. Leaders who pursue game-changers have no patience for the status quo—they focus their efforts on shattering the status quo.

Game-Changers refuse to allow their organizations to adopt conventional orthodoxy and bureaucracy—they challenge norms, break conventions, and they encourage diversity of thought. The message here is a simple one—don't copy, create. Don't just play the game—change the game. The goal is to create, improve on, and innovate around best practices in order to find *next* practices.

Develop A Clear Purpose

Leaders who create or inspire game changers are nothing if not aware. Not only are they self-aware, they're aware of the emotions and needs of others, and they are also clearly aware of what will be embraced in the market. They possess a refined blend of intrinsic curiosity and extrinsic focus. Perhaps, most of all, game-changing leaders are in touch with a greater purpose—they understand the value of serving beyond themselves.

If you want to create a real game-changer, have a purpose that serves, improves, helps, and inspires.

I would like to share with you the acronym for SMARTS. (**S**imple-**M**eaningful-**A**ctionable-**R**elational-**T**ransfomational-**S**calable)

Simple - While not all game-changers are simple, the best ones usually are. It was Albert Einstein who said, "If you can't explain it simply, you don't understand it well enough." In most cases, simple can be translated as realistic, cost effective, quick to adopt, and fast to implement. Don't get entangled in complexities—become heavily invested in simplicity.

Meaningful – Game-changers have great purpose, meet a need, solve a problem, serve an existing market, or create a new one—they are meaningful. Most leaders get sucked down into the weeds and spend too much of their valuable time majoring in the minors. If it's not really meaningful, if it doesn't serve a greater purpose, if it's not a game-changer, why do it? Ideas, products, services, and/or solutions that focus on value creation fare better than those that don't.

Actionable - It's not a game-changer if whatever "it" is never gets off the drawing board. If you can't turn an idea into innovation, if you can't put thought into practice, then it's not a game-changer. By definition, game-changers happen, they exist, they have life. They don't lurk in the shadowlands of the ethereal and esoteric; they become reality.

Relational - I have found game-changers enhance, extend, and leverage existing relationships, as well as serve to create new ones.

When you get down to brass tacks, all business boils down to people, and people mean relationships.

Real game-changers understand the power of people and relationships, and they embody this in both their construction and implementation. If you forget the people, you cannot have a game-changer.

Transformational - I have yet to see a static game-changer. By definition, a game-changer causes change. If nothing changes, if nothing is created, if nothing is improved, if nothing is transformed, then you don't have a game-changer. A lesson that I learned long ago is that you simply cannot experience sustainable improvement without transformation.

Scalable - If it's not scalable, it's not a game-changer. An idea that offers no hope of a future will more often than not turn into a nightmare rather fulfill a dream. True game-changers are built with velocity and sustainability in mind. The best thing about real game-changers is they build upon themselves to catalyze other accretive opportunities.

So, there you have it—now that I've shared my thoughts on creating game-changers, my SMARTS, if you will, it's your turn to share. This information can be a game-changer to many people if those who read it are willing to share their collective wisdom.

Chapter Nine: Innovative Game Changer Technologies

In both the consumer and business worlds, technology is constantly and rapidly evolving. Unique and innovative new business, health, and consumer technologies are emerging every day, but sometimes it takes a little time for the "next big thing" to get recognized and catch on.

Here are the innovative game-changing technologies that helped shape our world today.

Quantum Computing

Quantum computing has already found niche applications today. In the past few years, more and more funding has become available to take quantum circuits into new arenas, including imaging, sensing and measuring.

Quantum computing is a game-changer because it changes the fundamental paradigm in how computation is delivered into many industries—and in the era of Big Data, computation is everything.

Devices that Balance Innovation and Privacy

The nature and uses of data collected via devices and its relation to privacy have been a focus of mine, and privacy has evolved in the past decade. The current COVID-19 crisis is a perfect example of our need to balance research, information, and personal protection. "Our current regulatory environment stifles innovation and does not protect the individual. It's a lose-lose proposition." - Hillit Meidar-Alfi.

Transformer Neural Network Architecture

The transformer neural network architecture has revolutionized natural language processing capabilities (e.g., BERT from Google and GPT-2 from OpenAI). Since 2017, Transformer networks have dramatically advanced performance on tasks ranging from speech recognition to answering questions.

"This technology has helped lower barriers to activities like personalized tutoring and AI-powered customer support." Mike Moniz, Circadence Corporation

WeChat

The WeChat app is huge in China. Think of WhatsApp, PayPal, FB, and LinkedIn all in one, plus more. "WeChat has a feature that allows you to shake your phone and it will automatically connect you with someone nearby and/or globally if they are shaking their phone at the same exact time." William Charles Lee, GQIT

Cloud-Based Automated UI Testing

"We been using Qentinel, a cloud-based UI testing framework based on robot framework. Qentinel makes testing easy for technical people, and we can add that to our build automation stack. Unit tests have always had the biggest bang for the buck. Qentinel might displace that."

-Patrick Emmons, DragonSpears, Inc.

Blockchain Security and Compliance Monitoring

The major uptick in cryptocurrency awareness and interest in 2017, when prices reached historic levels, resulted in the need for blockchain security and compliance monitoring to rapidly evolve.

"These technologies and tools often work in the background (unknown to many) but are crucial in safeguarding blockchain platforms as well as in identifying fraud, anti-money laundering and compliance issues." - Jason Lau, Crypto.com

AutoAI

Most people have heard of AI, but most people don't know about AutoAI, deep learning and reinforcement specifically, and how transformational that has been to the industry. It's a game-changer because it democratizes model building to a much broader audience, allowing simple model building and accelerating the pace of AI adoption.

Remote Conditioning Monitoring

Most people don't know how huge of an impact technologies that allow for remote conditioning monitoring can have. Sensors that you can secure to equipment can tell a plant manager when the temperature is too high in critical spots where food is stored.

"Predictive maintenance technologies are changing the workforce and empowering technicians to prevent "firefighting" activities before they occur."- Ryan Chan, UpKeep Maintenance Management

These were a few I mentioned regarding each technological game-changer has been a successful benefit.

Chapter Ten: Historical Game-Changers in Stem Fields

In this final chapter, we are going to take a look at how these prominent people has made an impact in being a game-changer in the field of stem cell research.

Here are a few Black women who have or who currently are changing the world of STEM and serve as motivation for other Black and Brown girls to pursue their interests in the same fields.

Dr. Mae C. Jamison, MD

Dr. Mae Jemison was born in Alabama and raised in Chicago. Growing up, her parents made her spend many hours in the library, reading about the sciences, which sparked her passion for STEM. The history maker attended Stanford University, where she earned a degree in chemical engineering.

In 1992 Mae Jemison became the first African American woman to ever go to space with the Endeavour mission.

Alexa Canady, MD

Dr. Alexa Canady grew up in Michigan. Her father was a dentist and her mother an educator. Dr. Canady's interest in science grew more intense after she participated in a pre-college program at the University of Michigan. In 1987 she became Chief of Neurosurgery at the Michigan Children Hospital until she retired in 2001. Dr. Canady returned to practice medicine part-time after learning her new community in Florida didn't have a practicing African American surgeon in pediatrics.

Marie M. Daly, PhD

Dr. Marie Daly was born in 1921 to a family who was dedicated to her education. Daly studied at Queens College and New York University, before becoming the first African American to earn a doctorate degree in chemistry (from Columbia University).

Majorie Lee Browne, PhD

In 1949 Dr. Majorie Browne was the third African American woman to earn a PhD in mathematics. Dr. Browne became one the first scientists to set up an electronic computer lab at a historically Black college in 1960.

Aprille J. Ericsson-Jackson, PhD

Aprille Ericsson-Jackson is a native of Brooklyn, New York. She attended Massachusetts Institute of Technology before attending graduate school at Howard University. She was the first African American woman to earn a PhD in Mechanical Engineering from Howard University. Also received a PhD in Engineering at NASA's Goddard Space Flight Center.

Dr. Ericsson-Jackson is also committed to educating and inspiring more African American students to pursue careers in STEM.

Lisette Titre

Lisette Titre is a video game designer and education curriculum consultant with over thirteen years of experience. Recently, she partnered with Soledad O'Brien to encourage more young girls to consider education and jobs in STEM.

The purpose of this book was to give you a view of being a game-changer from a different perspective. My question to you is, do you have what it takes to make a difference, becoming a positive impact, and willing to change the game?

Game-Changers in Medicine:
Dr. Howard Hiatt

During his initial years as chief of medicine, the staff of Beth Israel as well as its board greeted his changes with enthusiasm. He was professional and knowledgeable, but he was also the kind of person to whom others are drawn. There was a charisma to Howard that helped make changes more acceptable to people. Other physicians, students, administrators, board members, and patients saw Howard with his smile and his easy, avuncular manner. He asked about staff members' families, and he did so remembering people's names and the names and ages of their kids. He was a rigorous manager, but an essential aspect of his management was to connect to people on a human level with warmth, collegiality, and often humor. His self-deprecating brand of off-the-cuff humor became one of his most appealing traits throughout the medical center.

As he worked his way through changes in the early days of his new role, Howard sought the advice of a number of friends and colleagues. In particular, he consulted Dr. Walter Bauer, chairman of the Department of Medicine at Mass General, who had selected excellent young doctors and sent a number of them to NIH for additional training before having them return to Mass General. Given Howard's interest in research, this approach very much appealed to him, and he would follow this model at the BI. "I looked for people who were accomplished clinically and very sophisticated scientifically and this was quite unusual," says Howard. A number of well-respected physicians at Beth Israel criticized Howard for this approach, arguing that the goal should be attracting superb clinicians regardless of their research interests or ability. All attention was owed to patients and their ailments, these people argued. But

Howardsaid it was important to take a broader view and that people who were both excellent physicians and accomplished researchers were more likely to identify the best treatments for patients.

As much as Howard loved his work at Beth Israel, he sometimes yearned to get back into the research laboratory. He had experienced the elation of success in the lab years earlier in his work on messenger RNA. There was no feeling quite like the sense of accomplishment that came with breaking new scientific ground. After five years as chief of medicine, with a strong team in place at Beth Israel, he decided the time was right to take a year's sabbatical and immerse himself in the lab. He felt instinctively that it would be impractical to do this in Boston—he knew that if he were on the BI property he would repeatedly be drawn into a wide variety of issues, meetings, decisions to be made. Thus, he took an opportunity to travel to Great Britain to work under a renowned cell biologist at the Imperial Cancer Research Fund Laboratory at Lincoln's Inn Fields in London, one of the world's leading cancer research centers.

Howard learned a great deal during his time working with the research scientists. His understanding of cancer deepened considerably.

His work in London also gave him an opportunity to become reacquainted with Dr. Brian Jarman, a general practitioner with a panel of patients mainly in a poor area of London. Many mornings, from nine to eleven, he would make house calls. The devotion to serving needy patients that Jarman brought to the work was clear. Beyond that, Howard was struck by the power of Jarman's intellect. Jarman's preparation for medicine had been quite unusual to say the least. He earned a PhD in geophysics at Cambridge and started out his professional career exploring the Sahara and other deserts for an oil company.

• • • • •

What began as a professional relationship between Howard and Jarman evolved into a close friendship between the two men that would stretch over almost six decades. Jarman would go on to become one of the leading primary care physicians in the United Kingdom, head of the Royal College of General Practitioners, and president of the British Medical Association.

The most lasting benefit for Howard from the year in London, in addition to his friendship with Brian, was the opportunity to see the delivery of ambulatory care by the men and women of the British National Health Service. Primary care was Jarman's specialty, and he guided Howard through the delivery system with a sense of mission and pride. Howard spent time with Jarman in inner-city London at a clinic serving many working and poor people. He also accompanied Brian on house calls. This effort on the part of Jarman and other NHS physicians to reach out and connect with people in need either through home or clinic visits impressed Howard. There was nothing like this at Beth Israel Hospital.

Thus did Howard become "aware of how much our Department of Medicine and American academic medicine in general were not doing, both internally within the hospitals and in surrounding neighborhoods." The National Health Service delivered care to any and all people regardless of their income or social standing and doing so in a setting convenient to the patient left an indelible mark.

Howard returned from London in 1970 with the images of the work he had observed Jarman doing fresh in his mind. He was determined that Beth Israel must do more to provide care to people in need within poor areas of the city of Boston. He also was determined to change the way care was delivered as well as the way the faculty was teaching medical students and residents. This was new ground. Medicine at the time was centered upon treating patients first and foremost and, only then, researching new treatments. Rarely did physicians talk about ways of improving the delivery of care or even what that delivery process should look like. There were standard models—one for ambulatory care and one for in-patient care—and rare was the deviation from these models.

Game-Changers in Breakthrough Medicine

In 1969, while Howard was in London, a radical new experiment in care delivery was launched by a team led by Dr. Robert Ebert, dean of Harvard Medical School. Ebert and his colleagues believed that the best way to deliver care would be through what he called a health maintenance organization (HMO): a group of physicians and other caregivers whose mission would be to keep its members healthy through prevention and early intervention and to provide excellent treatment to those members when they became sick. This HMO model was designed as well to provide care at a lower cost than traditional health insurance plans. Harvard funded this not-for-profit venture, which opened its doors in 1969. From the start, Harvard Community Health Plan attracted talented, idealistic doctors, but its initial efforts to attract subscription-paying members did not fare particularly well. At the start, a grand total of eighty-eight people signed up. Over time, however, the plan flourished.

Ebert also wished to link the new initiative to Harvard teaching hospitals, which Howard thought made perfect sense. Harvard Community Health Plan was unusual for many reasons, not the least of which was its experimental nature. Medicine was then and remains today a conservative profession. Change in healthcare organizations … can be both slow and painful. There is often a predisposition among powerful people in healthcare—including many doctors—to reflexively resist change. Howard recognized, however, that the largely hospital-based model of care was insufficient to meet the needs of many patients in a variety of parts of the community. "What was needed," Howard observed in his memoir, "was a capability within our Department of Medicine to study existing patterns of primary care: How was our society delivering care to people whose medical needs did not require hospitalization?"

• • • • •

The result of all this was the creation of the Beth Israel Ambulatory Care program, which connected patients with a primary care physician and provided ongoing care to patients via an ambulatory care center at the hospital. Howard was guided and inspired in this work by what he had seen in London. Beyond the ambulatory care center and mindful of Jarman's work in London, Howard established a relationship between Beth Israel and Dimock Community Health Center in the Roxbury neighborhood of Boston. This was a largely black neighborhood with a good deal of poverty and many health challenges ranging from chronic diseases to gun violence.

Howard was so taken by the work Jarman was doing that he later wrote a column that was published on the op-ed page of the *New York Times* (November 16, 1991) entitled "Meet Dr. Jarman. He makes house calls." The article contrasted the efficiency of the National Health Service with the wasteful nature of delivery in the United States (recounting the story of an elderly man who wanted very much to remain home but who was hospitalized for a series of tests that proved to be not at all helpful medically but nonetheless very expensive). Howard wrote that "Dr. Jarman says that in England ... the continuity of care by general practitioners ... means more prevention and fewer unnecessary procedures, hospitalizations, visits to consultants and costs."

Primary care could do so much more to improve care and control costs but in the United States just 25 percent of physicians are in primary care, while in the UK it is half of all doctors, where their income is on a par with that of heart or brain surgeons. The relationship between primary care doctor and patient is central to the ability of caregivers in the UK to provide ongoing care responsive to patients' overall needs.

The Success of a Game-Changer

Game-changers are those who appear in history books as having not only stepped outside the box but took it a step further and blew the entire side of the box out. They are the business minds, owner, and entrepreneurs who inspire an entire population and country. When asked your greatest driving force it might be the name of a great business owner who has made an impact on how you do, and think, about business as a whole.

These are the people we label as game-changers in business. We asked entrepreneurs and business owners who they felt the biggest game changers in history were.

Some great game-changers spend less time trying to find out how to make something cheaper and instead focus on making an item much, much better. Executive coach Michael Harden comments on his pick for a game-changer. "There is no doubt that Steve Jobs has to be at the top of this list. He either started or revolutionized at least six different industries. He was able to do this because he was a non-linear thinker.

Rather than thinking about how to take something and incrementally make it better, like many CEOs do, he would make a quantum leap.

Instead of spending time and money trying to figure out how to make a cell phone better or cheaper, or how to improve on the "Walkman" and other handheld recording/playing devices, he looked at it from a different perspective: What would I do if I had to design or create this kind of device today? He had to "unlearn" what we all knew and assumed about these devices, and start from scratch. That non-linear thinking, which is very absent with a lot of executives today, is what allowed him to create such revolutionary products and start brand-new markets. Who knew they needed a smart phone before he showed us the iPhone? Who thought they needed a hand-held tablet before he introduced us to the iPad?

There are also game-changers which have been left out of the general conversation when it comes to the well-known list. Matt Reischer, Esq., nominates one such person. "The founder of Marvel Comics Stan 'The Man' Lee is an underappreciated visionary for changing the marketplace of comic book publishing and pushing the boundary of the comic medium. I have always admired Stan Lee's ability to sell while not seeming to sell by creating a believable narrative that grips the imagination. The ability to effortlessly sell through persuasion and narrative story telling is a business skill that resonates for me as a lawyer. While Stan's contribution may not appear to be game changing because the genre of superheroes and funny books are often chided for not being serious, no one can deny that the contemporary pop culture milieu is a $20 Billion business encompassing Movies, TV, and video games."

Some business owners change the game with how they run their business instead of what they do with their business. Author Kevin Paul Scott feels this makes a game-changer. "A CEO that really changed the game was Truett Cathy, the founder and former CEO of Atlanta-based Chick-fil-A. Cathy's relentless commitment to quality and customer service set his company apart. In 8 Essential Exchanges, I emphasize the need for leaders to exchange expedience for excellence. Truett Cathy embodied that exchange and once said, 'We need to get better before we get bigger; once we get better our customers will demand that we get bigger.' Chick- fil-A recently stole the chicken crown from KFC, becoming the U.S. revenue leader for a quick-service restaurant chicken company."

No matter which game-changer you find inspiration from the entire group could be described as, in general, what you should aspire to be. Game-changers make business fun. Dreaming about products that could make a huge impact on the market and a difference in how people live is like dreaming of winning the lottery. Until you reach that point, admiring game-changers of past and present will make you want to get up and go.

Epilogue: Living the Dream, My Personal Success Story

Living the Dream: My Personal Success Story

Written by: Mr. Oscar J. Starr III

In this day in age, we all have used the old adage in what we call "living the dream." This particular phrase is often but somewhat used in when we are greeting each other every day, either through passing or meeting people in whom we come in contact. But what does living the dream mean to you? Are you saying it just because it sounds good and you want to impress those people around you? However, to you that the term "living the dream" can have so much meaning, and don't realize that it can carry so much weight.

Let me share something with you for a moment and maybe you'll come to a clear understanding as to why you feel is important to be living the dream and having a real story to backup what you're saying. To me, living the dream doesn't mean that I was born into an affluent family with a wealthy background, nor was I given a trust fund in my name. I had come from very humble beginnings in which that I didn't have much growing up; however, I shared a bedroom with my younger brother, and we often shared a bed as well. To make a long story short, I had grown up to be a responsible hardworking man that one day I had a dream in wanting to become successful. I can remember when I was in the eighth grade, my teacher had spoken prophetically into my life. Her name is Mrs. Sandra McGee-Horton; she always had believed in me and knew I had potential to be successful. I will never forget that day when she had written a note on a back of a picture. "To Oscar, a suave and debonair young man who is destined for greatness." Those words resonated and stuck with me for a very longtime, and I'll never forget what she has spoken over my life.

I've had my share of living from pillar to post, having my cars repossessed, and was homeless, staying at a shelter for at least six months. Trying to do my best in getting back on my feet, especially when you have a wife and daughter you're trying your best to support. However, let's fast forward to the present day, okay? Over the past several years, I've attempted to become an entrepreneur, in which didn't work out so well in the end.

As time went on, I've learned from my failures and decided to put my dream on hold for a very long time. Was I disappointed in myself by not doing it right the first time? The answer is yes, because I wanted to fast track everything, without going about conducting the proper research, failed to be educated in what it had taken to be an entrepreneur and so on.

As of September 2019, that is when I became inspired by my former employer, in which whom I connected, through his words of encouragement. That was the day I decided and had the drive to become an entrepreneur one more time. This time things were going to be different and it's a whole new approach. God has blessed me with the vision along with a creative mind in writing down a business plan.

This wonderful idea was passed on to my fiancé, in whom she was showing her support without any reservation or negativity. By which she had given her insight as well as brought new ideas to the table. We discussed what the plans were, and we started from there.

That is when I also decided to take my time and do in-depth research, investigate as well as read and educate myself in how to be an entrepreneur. I realize that it takes much work, patience, and most of all, time, in order to build a new business or company. From that day forward, I began to build our website as well as had an idea on how it was going to be formatted. Second, I also constructed and written a business plan, in which this time had all the details needed.

Each day, I would take the time while I was at my current job to work on building our new company. Constantly gaining input and reading success stories, etc. As of now, we been blessed to have new networking connections with various business professionals and will be attending business events.

As I continue to build our new company, I will have this desirable hunger to be successful, by taking this one day at a time. Today, I am more encouraged and inspired than ever before, in which taking small steps that's going to take me places that I can even imagine. I'm excited in what's happening right now, and yes, I'm ready to launch this new company. Today, we have a new online store platform in which several products are featured. Our online store will feature and showcase various office products, office equipment, school supplies, and finally, electronics which feature Apple products etc. I'm excited in what our new company is about to become, but nevertheless, I'm blessed beyond total measure. One of things I do know is that building the company will come with many obstacles and hurdles along the way. Needless to say, I'm not going to allow any of those get in my way, because one thing that I will do is fly high above and keep soaring.

We also have several professional social networking pages, Facebook, Instagram, and also Linked-in, etc. But most of all, our business website is reaching higher numbers each day, as well as our Facebook business page.

As I conclude, let me say that to me living the dream isn't about me obtaining riches nor chasing money, but it's about the real support from your friends and people who have your back and show it through action. Living the dream isn't about giving up or throwing in the towel, which is when you get up, dust off, and keep fighting and pushing.

Living the dream is when you have a very supportive significant other, that's going to always be there for you when others trying to speak negatively about you or your new company. The purpose of this is to inspire and encourage and to change your thinking the next time you hear someone say that they're "living the dream."

Whether you know it or not, everyone has a backstory to tell when it comes to speaking about their own rags-to-riches success story. I don't consider myself as someone to be another interest story; however, I wanted to tell my story and to share with those who desire to become successful one day. Before I end this summation, allow me to introduce myself.

My name is Oscar J. Starr III, and I am the new and upcoming entrepreneur and business owner. I am the Founder and Owner of the newly formed Express Direct Professional Services, LLC. I am also the author of my newest book entitled *Keys to Creating a Small Business: Your Personal Guide to Success.*

Even today, I am thankful for the people who was in my life and being a blessing also. To my parents who had seen potential in me, even when I couldn't see it for myself, and they encouraged me to stay in school and not give up.

The Co-founder and President of Operations is my fiancée, Ms. Danielle Ayers, who has brought so many ideas and wonderful insight in which will make our company a glowing success like other. We are going to be an innovation in being game-changers in the industry of customer service. What is your personal success story that's going to be a blessing to someone? Are you living the dream just to have it all to yourself, or are you willing to give back and pay it forward? One should have the continuing drive and the insatiable hunger to be successful. Don't ever starve or deprive yourself from reaching for opportunities. I am also the Founder/Creator of the new #GameChangers clothing brand.

While you're building and working on establishing your company or business, be willing to help someone along the way by expressing and exemplifying selflessness. Finally, being an entrepreneur or business owner is going to require a test of patience, hard-work, endurance, and unfailing dedication.

You may encounter detours, perhaps roadblocks along the way, but you to got to KEEP GOING and GO FOR IT. NEVER THROW IN THE TOWEL.

www.ingramcontent.com/pod-product-compliance
Lightning Source LLC
Chambersburg PA
CBHW051336150726
47997CB00004B/1485